OFFICIAL
FORTNITE
BATTLE ROYALE
SURVIVAL GUIDE

LEARN HOW TO SURVIVE BATTLE ROYALE

While Fortnite continues to evolve with you, the community, it's still important to get your head around key areas of the game. Here we'll give you the inside info that will help you develop as a player. If you want to discover new ways to dazzle your friends and dominate in battle then look no further.

BEFORE YOU BEGIN

BECAUSE THE BATTLE BEGINS BEFORE YOU BOARD THE BUS

The fun starts when the Battle Bus begins dropping eager players onto the island. There's the desperate dash to avoid the Storm and the ever-present threat from other opponents. Eventually, only one player can be left standing. This is Fortnite. While these basics remain the same, the route to victory is forever changing. There's no one way to rule—that's half the fun of it! Still, there's a lot to learn if you want to survive Fortnite's intense PvP action, improve your tenacity in combat, and upgrade your building skills to rule with ease. We will cover it all in this Survival Guide. But, before you begin, here are some key tips and tricks.

ALTER YOUR CONTROLS

Fortnite comes equipped with a number of pre-set control configurations. It is, however, worth making a few adjustments in the Options menu once you have settled into a preferred play style. Earning a Victory Royale isn't easy, but there's no reason your fingers can't be comfortable while you try.

THE SOLDIER

If you enjoy getting eliminations, you may want to try the Combat Pro configuration. This setup is designed for those of you who prefer an experience focused around intensive PvP combat.

THE BUILDER

Builder Pro is designed to help those who love to spend their time building. It maps specific build pieces to the triggers on a controller, which is perfect for those eager to create elaborate structures as quickly as possible.

THE RUNNER

The Quick Build configuration is for those of you who like to whip up structures while on the move. Forget about complex designs, this is for players who want to build on the go.

ADJUST YOUR SENSITIVITY

Make Fortnite more comfortable by tinkering with the sensitivity of either your thumbsticks or your mouse. Every player is different and works at different speeds, so why not try altering the X- and Y-axis sensitivity ever so slightly between games until you find a setting that makes you happy.

CHECK YOUR MATCHMAKING REGION

It's worth double-checking that you are playing in the correct Matchmaking Region before entering a round of Fortnite. You can do this from the Options menu before you begin a game. Be on the lookout for the lowest ping number to obtain the smoothest experience possible.

PROTECT YOUR ACCOUNT

There are many ways to rule at Fortnite, but you can't put any of your plans into action if you can't access your account. Protect yourself by activating Two-Factor Authentication (2FA). Go to your Account Settings, click Password & Security, and look for the Two-Factor Authentication heading. Keep your account safe and remember, Epic employees will never ask for your password!

BE RESPECTFUL TO ONE ANOTHER

Everybody comes to Fortnite to have a good time, and that means every member of the community should do their best to be respectful and inclusive. The great thing about Fortnite is that anybody and everybody can play, so be kind and courteous to each and every player that you come across.

JOIN THE WIDER COMMUNITY

With so much happening in the world of Fortnite it can be difficult to keep track, and that's why we encourage anybody interested in the game to jump in and engage with the wider community on Twitter (@FortniteGame), Instagram (@Fortnite), Facebook (@FortniteGame), and YouTube (Fortnite). We love to hear from our players, and this is definitely the best way to make your voice heard!

STAY UP TO DATE WITH THE LATEST CHANGES

Remember, Fortnite is constantly evolving and that means elements of the game are subject to change at any time. If you really want to rule at Fortnite, you should check out the latest news on the game at the Official Fortnite Blog (Fortnite.com) which covers all of the latest patch notes and updates.

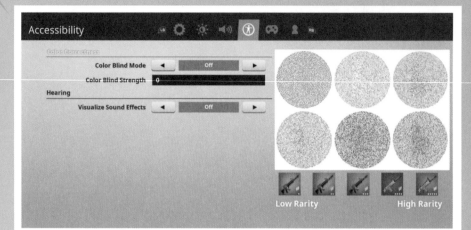

USE THE ACCESSIBILITY OPTIONS

Remember, Fortnite has robust accessibility features should you need them. You can find these in the Options menu; there's a variety of selections that will allow color-blind players to adjust color correction, while those with a hearing impairment will be able to visualize audio effects via a radial indicator for sound.

REPORT PLAYERS IF YOU NEED TO

If you find that there is a player, or a group of players, out there trying to spoil the fun for everyone else, you can always report them by hitting the pause button in-game, selecting Feedback and then the player in question, prompting Epic to investigate. Fortnite is, above all else, about community and inclusivity.

HOW TO LEVEL UP QUICKLY

GET THE BATTLE PASS

If you want to earn more XP and earn cool exclusive seasonal items, you'll want to sign up for the Battle Pass.

COMPLETE CHALLENGES

Boost your Battle Pass tier by getting Battle Stars, earned by completing Battle Pass and Daily Challenges.

USER BEWARE!

The Item Shop rotates its stock every 24 hours, so you'll want to check it every time that you log in so you don't miss something awesome.

KEEP AT IT

If you want to keep earning XP, you are going to need to keep playing: The longer you can last on the island the better.

TRY NEW GAME MODES

Limited Time Modes are always changing so be sure to check what's available before you board that bus.

POINTS OF INTEREST

A BRIEF TOUR AROUND THE ISLAND

You're about to get a crash course in some of the island's hottest spots. Get involved in the tussle at Tilted Towers, skulk around in the shadows of Haunted Hills, or try chilling out at Paradise Palms with your buddies. One way or another, you're guaranteed to find

a destination to suit your preferred play style somewhere on the island. While the map will constantly change, a lot of the key locales generally remain the same, so maximize your options by getting your head round the major places of interest before you drop in. In this section, you will find eight places of interest that will help any aspiring player get one over on the competition—but remember, it's always worth venturing off into other named and unnamed corners of the island to see what surprises are in store.

FIGHT TO SURVIVE
You and your friends should aim to drop into the middle of Tilted Towers if you are eager for action.

TILTED TOWERS

Where chaos reigns supreme

▶ **COORDINATES: D6**

▶ **COMMON MATERIAL: STONE**

If you want to put your survival and combat skills to the test, you're going to want to consider landing at this bustling early-game hotspot. This is the area of the island where chaos can reign supreme; Tilted Towers is carnage from the get-go, a trial by fire where only the most skilled players will make it out with their loot alive. Not only is this the place to be if you want a crash course in the punishing realities of Battle Royale, it's also an excellent location to develop your improvisational abilities. Get your boots on the ground and quickly scramble for cover; Tilted Towers is where your combat and survival skills will be put to the test.

PURE CHAOS
Tilted Towers favors the bold, so you'll want to try and get your hands on an offensive weapon as fast as possible if you want to survive.

USER BEWARE!

Expect to find that the island evolves over time, elements of the locations changing with the seasons.

LOOK TO THE NORTH

Once you've looted the lake, you should either plan to head north to the motel or west to the factory, unless you fancy heading south to involve yourself in the chaos of Tilted Towers.

BE ON THE LOOKOUT
Consider landing near the edges. You'll be exposed, but if you're lucky enough to find a long-range rifle here, you can take enemies by surprise.

LOOT LAKE

The epicenter of it all

▶ **COORDINATES: E4**

▶ **COMMON MATERIAL: WOOD**

In many respects, Loot Lake has it all. Sitting at the center of the island, this area will provide you with an abundance of action and excitement from the moment your boots hit the ground. Thanks to the surrounding woodlands, there are plenty of resources to harvest here, all of which will help you to put down your first structures in a round. Oh, and then there's the loot to collect too—it's not named Loot Lake for nothing. This locale has drastically evolved and changed since the game began, making it one of the most exciting destinations on the island to head towards if you want to witness Fortnite's ever-evolving narrative. It's a great place to drop if you're unsure of where to go, or you're just starting out.

MINE AWAY
Be sure to grab as many resources here as you possibly can before the mid game begins.

PLEASANT PARK
A pleasant place to park yourself

▶ **COORDINATES: C3**
▶ **COMMON MATERIAL: WOOD**

Come for the loot; stay for the resources; alert everybody in the surrounding area to your presence by enjoying a nice, carefree game of soccer. This is the type of location that, should you enjoy being super sneaky, you could easily spend most of a round exploring—if you're lucky enough to avoid being in the path of the Storm. If you're looking for easy loot, you should try to check each of the attics as you move between the houses—this is where chests are usually hidden away. Once you are content with your item haul, look to either fortify a location that offers good lines of sight—giving you the opportunity to pick off enemies at range—or aim to move to the next key place of interest on the island.

THE BEAUTIFUL GAME
The soccer field is a great place to relieve a little tension between you and your squad, but it does leave groups devastatingly open to attacks.

POINTS OF INTEREST

ALL HAIL THE LLAMA
North of Haunted Hills, near Junk Junction, is this impressive (and very distracting) Llama statue. Nobody knows why it's there but it contains some pretty decent loot!

PRAY FOR LOOT
While there are chests on the top and middle floors of the church, you should land on the ground floor and break down through it. There's a chance of secret chest spawn in the basement.

HAUNTED HILLS

Embrace your fears in the name of survival

▶ **COORDINATES: B3**

▶ **COMMON MATERIAL: STONE**

There is no reason to be afraid of Haunted Hills. Okay, so is it a creepy area complete with a dilapidated church, a mysterious Llama statue, and an old graveyard? It sure is! But it's also an area that very few people choose to land at from the Battle Bus. Try using Haunted Hills as the place to practice sneaking through the shadows—just remember to crouch for maximum impact! Be sure to take a look south of the church, as there you will find a small building that's likely housing good loot and a rare vending machine spawn. Also, be on the lookout for random vehicles on the roadside: The pickup trucks will often contain chests. Haunted Hills is a great place for the player looking for an easy-going start to any round of Fortnite.

WAILING WOODS

A place to practice building

▶ **COORDINATES: I3**

▶ **COMMON MATERIAL: WOOD**

There are few places on the island better equipped to let you practice building in peace than Wailing Woods. While it's true that the woods have changed and evolved with each passing season, it's still a location that is positively plush with resources to harvest. There's a huge forest here just waiting to be introduced to your Harvesting Tool, making it a perfect spot to gather wood and practice building structures like the all-important 1x1 box and tower. Of course, there's still plenty more to see and do here if you're already comfortable laying down structures. Spend a little time exploring and you'll no doubt come across the bunker at the center of the woods which contains a four-way teleporter—making it easier than ever to come here for early game looting before ducking out unscathed to head to new points of interest across the island.

SO MANY RESOURCES
A lot has changed at Wailing Woods, but its bountiful array of resources never has. This is a great location to come to in the early game to get well prepared for what comes next!

THE LABS
At the heart of Wailing Woods you should expect to encounter science labs and a bunker. While this space is always evolving, it tends to be pretty great for getting your hands on some solid loot.

USER BEWARE!
Try and take the time to explore every corner of the island. Use the Battle Pass Challenges to help guide you to new points of interest every week.

DANGER AROUND EVERY CORNER

Be prepared to put up a tough fight to claim Snobby's loot. Thankfully, the shores are full of great cover and vantage points for players.

SNOBBY SHORES

Fight for your right to get all of that loot

▶ **COORDINATES: A5**

▶ **COMMON MATERIAL: STONE**

You have probably noticed that the route that the Battle Bus takes across the island changes every game. Because of this, it would be wise to weigh up the likely risk/reward of landing in a particular area. Snobby Shores can, for example, be a tough spot to survive should it be one of the first named locations that the Battle Bus reaches. Should it appear towards the end of the route, however, you may just find that many players ignore it, making it an excellent location to gear up in preparation of a mid-game tussle. The area is made up of five houses, each of which sits within its own walled grounds—if you spot another player it's possible to keep a low profile, get your hands on some tasty loot, and get away unseen. If you're feeling particularly courageous why not try accessing the houses to the south; one of these has a hidden basement that contains at least three chests.

PLAN YOUR ROUTE

If you come through here but aren't able to find an ATK, why not try heading north to the super villain base or south to the Viking Village?

SMARTY PANTS

Enter the science labs if it seems quiet. There are two chest chances in the larger structure, while the blue mushrooms will give your shield a boost.

DUSTY DIVOT

Changing with the times

▶ **COORDINATES: F5**

▶ **COMMON MATERIAL: WOOD**

Back in the olden days, Dusty Divot was known to all as the Dusty Depot—three warehouses surrounded by flat land. Ever since the meteor blew it all to bits in Season 4, it's now one-and-a-half depots and a massive crater. But with destruction comes new life, and the divot is currently teeming with woodland amid loot-filled abandoned science labs. This is the sort of area where you will need to adjust your strategy to reflect the terrain. Landing in a ditch would usually leave you open to attacks from those up on higher ground, but thanks to all those trees around you, your opponents may find that hitting you from above suddenly isn't as easy as it seems. Approach Dusty Divot with caution, use the cover to your advantage, and try to farm as many materials as you can before other players descend on the area—or lie in wait and get some cheeky eliminations!

HARVEST RESOURCES RESPONSIBLY

Every time you harvest an element of the map it will indicate to other players that you've been in the area. Consider gathering a little material from a lot of places to reduce your footprint.

USER BEWARE!

If you're playing with your buddies you should try and remember to use map markers. It's an easy way to keep your group together.

RACE FOR GLORY
Venture north of Paradise Palms and you'll find a racetrack, which is pretty cool. If that isn't your speed, try heading south to find a loot-filled town, junkyard, and garage.

PARADISE PALMS

Fun and fear go hand in hand

▶ **COORDINATES: I8**

▶ **COMMON MATERIAL: METAL**

Paradise Palms is the place to be if you want to blow off some steam. This sandy deathtrap will give you a good opportunity to put your skills to the test and rack up a few eliminations, but there's far more to do and see here should you be so inclined. There's the scrap yard that's perfect for gathering resources, there's the dinosaur—perfect for snapping a quick group photo with your squad—and then there's the racetrack, a great place to mess around with your friends and enjoy some fun with other players you've met out on the island. Paradise Palms is certainly dangerous, but it's filled with a variety of items, resources and opportunities that can help you have fun—outside of eliminating other players in your ever-present search for a Victory Royale!

MOVE WITH EASE
The white tower is a deathtrap. It's full of excellent loot, so it's a magnet for every other player in the vicinity. If you make it out of here alive, you'll be a Fortnite legend.

SURVIVING THE STORM

HOW TO USE THE CIRCLE TO YOUR ADVANTAGE

With 100 players all vying for victory, it can sometimes be too easy to forget that there's a Storm closing in around the island. Every few minutes your space to maneuver on the map becomes a little bit tighter, funneling all active players a little closer together for some truly spectacular battles. One of the worst ways to fall in Fortnite is to get caught outside of the circle, and that's why we've collected the very best tips and advice on how you can avoid the Storm, and even use it to your advantage against other players.

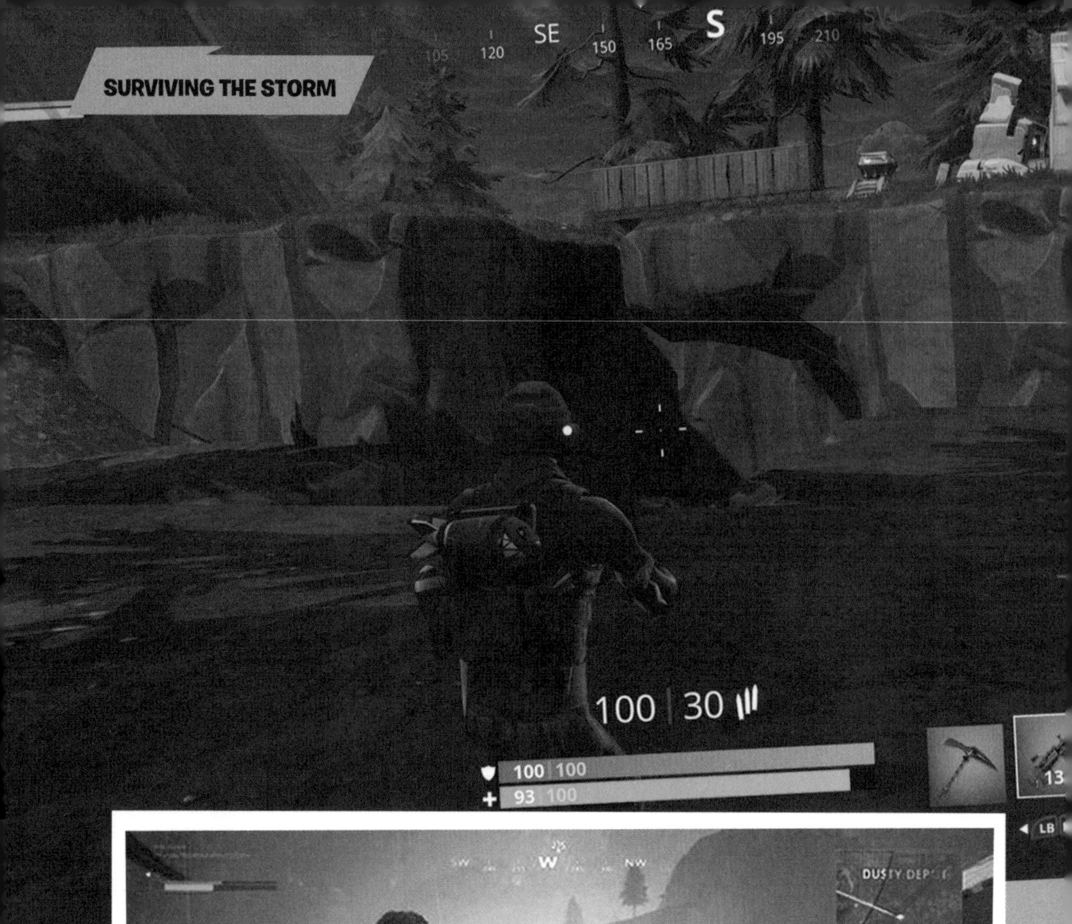

SE · S

105 · 120 · 150 · 165 · 195 · 210

100 | 30

100 | 100
93 | 100

13

LB

W · NW

DUSTY DEPOT

0:25 · 14 · 0

90 · 30 · 27

50 100
43 100

THE EYE OF THE STORM

One minute after the Battle Bus finishes crossing the island, successfully dropping all 100 players off, the first Storm Circle will appear. From that point onward, the circle will begin to shrink at specific intervals, the danger increasing with it—get caught inside the Storm, and it'll start chipping away at your health.

KEEP MOVING

Once you've landed safely on the island, secured a weapon, and skillfully dodged the first wave of other players, you may want to start thinking ahead to the arrival of the Storm. You'll have quite a bit of time to prepare, so there's no need to rush. Keep moving, gather resources, look out for better loot, and consider avoiding confrontation for as long as you can.

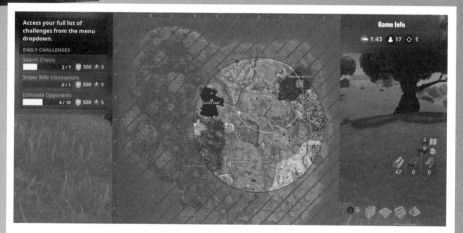

ANTICIPATE ITS DIRECTION

The first five times the circle shrinks, you'll be able to anticipate the location it is closing around, giving you the opportunity to pull up the map and consider the best route to safety. Once the Storm reaches the sixth closure, however, the circle will begin sweeping slowly across the map, which marks the beginning of the end game.

USER BEWARE!

Vehicles are excellent at helping you escape the Storm, but be wary of the amount of noise they generate.

DON'T RISK IT

You might think that just because you have a healthy supply of Med Kits and Bandages you'll be able to survive the Storm. Now, while this may indeed be true at its earliest incarnations, once it shrinks for a fifth time you'll find that it becomes increasingly difficult. Dip in and out of the Storm if you need to, but be aware of your health at all times.

CAMP THE EDGE

It can be a viable tactic to camp out at the edge of the Storm. In doing this, you'll have the opportunity to catch any players that are desperately trying to make it to safety in early and mid game. When the circle gets really tight, and the player count starts dwindling, it becomes increasingly unlikely that you'll be attacked from behind—try using this positioning to your advantage in the end game.

DON'T PANIC

Should you find yourself inside the Storm, try not to panic. Take a second to bring up your map and work out the fastest straight-line route to safety. Try utilizing ramps to get you up to higher ground and bridge large gaps with flat floor pieces to speed up traversal. If you're really stuck, take a second to use a healing item—Bandages or Med Kit—to ensure you have enough health to make it out alive.

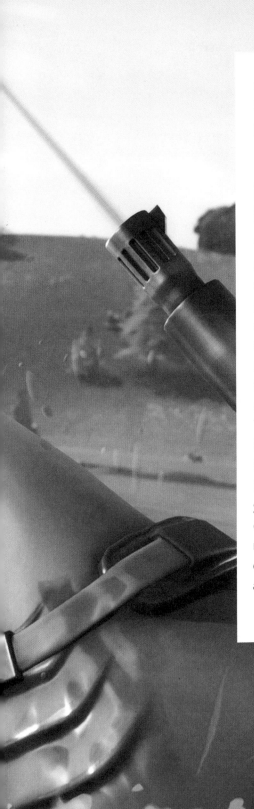

SURVIVAL TACTICS

BATTLE IT OUT UNTIL THE BITTER END

To succeed you first need to survive. The only way to lay claim to a Victory Royale is to be the last player standing, although the way in which you approach such a feat can take many different forms. You play the game your way and don't let anybody compromise your style. That said, there are some Battle Royale basics it's worth taking on board before heading out to the island. These survival skills will give you a better understanding of the different strategies that may help you at various stages of the game, giving you a vital advantage over your adversaries.

HOW TO SURVIVE THE EARLY GAME

Your first test in Fortnite comes as soon as you are corralled onto the Battle Bus. The direction it moves over the island changes every round, so try to be flexible when deciding when and where to jump. Landing in a named location will likely yield better loot, but it'll also increase your chances of bumping into other players. Isolated spots may mean you fill out your inventory slower but it may be safer. Wherever you decide to land, try to keep these three basic tips in mind:

DON'T HESITATE

The moment your feet hit the floor, you should probably be moving. Get out of the open and get yourself a weapon, keeping an eye out for other players as you do. With 99 others out there trying to survive, the early game can get pretty frantic, pretty quickly.

EYES ON THE PRIZE

It's always important to monitor your surroundings. If you see construction on the horizon, move with caution. If you spot another player, consider whether you have enough gear to get the upper hand. Fortnite is a game of seizing good opportunities, after all.

EASE INTO CONFRONTATIONS

One awesome thing about Fortnite is that you can decide how you want to play and how you want to win. But you can't win if you've been eliminated. Consider engaging players in combat as a last resort in the early game.

USER BEWARE!

Try wearing headphones while playing and use the subtle audio cues to give you a better sense of what's around you.

COLLECT RESOURCES

It's easy to get caught up in all the looting as you search for a great weapon, but don't forget to grab resources with your Harvesting Tool too. Building is an important strategy in Fortnite and to build you're going to need a healthy supply of wood, stone and metal to begin crafting structures.

KEEP UP WITH THE STORM

Unless you want to get eliminated by the Storm, you really should keep one eye on the clock under the mini-map. This will let you know how long you have left until the circle starts shrinking; try to leave yourself enough time to plan your route ahead and, critically, to get yourself to safety.

HOW TO SURVIVE THE MID GAME

LOOK OUT FOR CONSUMABLES ▶

Every consumable item has its advantages. You'll want to be on the lookout for Bandages and Med Kits to keep your health bar looking, well, healthy; Shield Potions will provide extra protection against gunfire; Slurp Juice and Chug Jugs can be vital for survival as they restore both your health and shield bars slowly over time.

LOOT SMARTLY

Players will drop everything they had in their backpack when they are eliminated. If you are happy with your loadout but eager to get the ammo and items, equip your Harvesting Tool and hit the action button over the area to swap your loadout without accidentally throwing your favorite gun down to the floor.

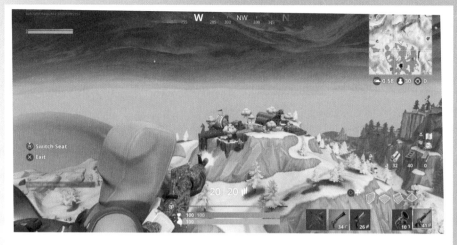

PICK YOUR BATTLES

When you see two players fighting you should consider waiting it out. If you watch the confrontation from a distance, you'll be able to better judge whether you should move on or move in to seize the elimination opportunity—and all of the loot!

SEIZE EVERY OPPORTUNITY

At this stage of the game, some players begin to find it difficult to avoid the Storm. Use this to your advantage; camp out on the edge of the circle (with your back against cover if you can) and play the waiting game. Players running for their lives are often too busy sweating it out to notice you sitting there ready to strike.

SURVIVING THE END GAME
THE LAST PLAYER STANDING WINS

PREPARE TO IMPROVISE

Improvising within the ever-shrinking circle is key, but so is sticking within your comfort zone. To survive this phase of the game you'll want to have a few structures you can build without fear or hesitation. You'll also understand the feel of your weapons, and be eagerly anticipating other players' movements.

ELEVATION IS EVERYTHING

Unless you're a great shot with a Sniper Rifle you aren't going to earn consistent Victory Royales without elevation. Getting higher than other players can be key to victory; many battles come down to who can get above the other faster. If you can't find elevation, go ahead and create some!

BUILDING IS SUPER IMPORTANT

LOOK FOR STRUCTURES

If you see a building on the horizon at this stage in the game, it's fairly likely to be hiding another player. Move with caution from this point on.

WEAK FOUNDATIONS

If you want to bring down a structure quickly, aim to destroy the bottom of it. Rockets, grenades, or Remote Explosives will get the job done.

USER BEWARE!

You can claim a Victory Royale without building a single structure in a game, but you'll need sharp reflexes and to be able to move deftly to pull it off.

BUILD QUICKLY

At this stage you will want to be building quickly and often. You should try to have 1,500 of each material with you, giving you plenty of options.

BUILD OFTEN

Building frequently is a key skill late in a game. A structure can be used as makeshift cover, as a trap, and as a way of scoping out new areas.

WEAPONS GUIDE

HOW TO BECOME MORE EFFECTIVE WITH YOUR WEAPONRY

While there are many routes to a Victory Royale, you will no doubt be wielding weapons to do it. Thankfully, there are weapons spread across the island—you just need to find them first. With a variety of weapon types and rarities to contend with, this is the section of the Survival Guide that breaks down the most important aspects of combat. From what guns you should look to pack your inventory with, to the best ways to wield an assault rifle, we've got you covered.

UNDERSTAND WEAPON RARITY

You've probably noticed that each of the weapons in Fortnite comes in a few colorful variations. That's because there are different rarities! While the base stats may stay the same, the damage output increases across the color spectrum. This is how that breaks down in-game:

◄ **ORANGE (LEGENDARY)**

These weapons offer a higher damage per second (DPS) to help you claim eliminations quickly and efficiently.

PURPLE (EPIC) ►

Only a handful of weapons will spawn as Epic or Legendary, but the ones that do are worth your full attention.

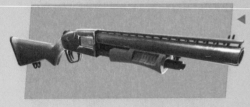

◄ **BLUE (RARE)**

Rare weapons are a good find and should be sought out as you look towards the middle and end game.

GREEN (UNCOMMON) ►

Get your hands on an Uncommon weapon and you should be prepared for just about anything on the island.

◄ **GRAY (COMMON)**

Gray weapons will likely be the first that you come across on the island. They are great for protecting yourself in a pinch.

RECYCLE YOUR WEAPONS

As the rarity of a weapon increases, so does its potential damage output. For example, if two players come up against each other wielding the same assault rifle, the player with the rarer weapon will enjoy a higher damage per second. It's worth keeping this in mind as you come across new weapons.

MOVE RESPONSIBLY

Unless you're using a shotgun, you should consider rooting yourself in place before engaging an enemy. Weapons such as the assault rifle, SMG, and sniper rifle are often more effective if you aren't moving and strafing. Instead, you should try centering yourself with your opponent, crouch down, and focus on shooting straight to claim that elimination.

BRING A HARVESTING TOOL TO A GUN FIGHT

If loot luck has not been with you, you can always pull out your Harvesting Tool and swing it at an opponent. But this is a risky proposition...While it has a low damage output, it can be the difference between life and elimination if you get caught needing to reload at a bad time. Remember, you need to use every tool in your arsenal, and be prepared to improvise, to survive!

USE MOVEMENT TO YOUR ADVANTAGE

Given that there are 99 other players around you on the island, each with different loadouts and skills, there's never one clear route to success. One thing every player does have in common, however, is their ability to move. Use this to your advantage, jumping in the middle of engagements to try and throw your enemies off; movement is key and can be one of your most effective tools!

CONSIDER ALL OF YOUR OPTIONS

Every weapon in Fortnite can be used to help you claim a Victory Royale. While it is true that some guns are better suited to certain situations, improvisation really is key to success. Build your own playstyle by using weapons in unconventional ways; bring a sniper rifle to a close-quarters battle, whip out a pistol at range, use an assault rifle as a battering ram. Fortune favors the bold, after all.

BE PREPARED

A QUICK GUIDE TO SOME OF FORTNITE'S MOST IMPORTANT WEAPON TYPES

SHOTGUNS

If you are looking for a weapon that can get you through just about any entanglement, you should get your hands on a shotgun. These come in three varieties: Pump, Tactical, and Heavy. You'll find that each of these weapons handles a little differently, so why not try dropping into the Playground or Creative modes to try them out before boarding that Battle Bus?

BE ON THE LOOKOUT FOR THE...

◄ LEGENDARY HEAVY SHOTGUN

Rarity: Legendary **Damage:** High
Magazine Size: Low **Reload Time:** Low
Damage Per Second: Medium

Thanks to its power, speed, and utility, the Legendary Heavy Shotgun is one of the most flexible shotguns available in the game.

ASSAULT RIFLES

If you are looking to claim some quick eliminations, scare enemies away from valuable loot, or attempting to bust a hole in a defensive perimeter, the Assault Rifle will get the job done. These weapons are readily available, offer a fast rate of fire and have a pretty incredible damage per second across the full-auto and burst shot variants. There are plenty of Assault Rifles to choose from in Fortnite, so be sure to give each of them a try to see which suits your play style the best.

BE ON THE LOOKOUT FOR THE...

◀ LEGENDARY ASSAULT RIFLE

Rarity: Legendary **Damage:** Low
Magazine Size: High **Reload Time:** Low
Damage Per Second: Medium

Difficult to come by for good reason, the Legendary Assault Rifle has best in class DPS, low recoil and incredible accuracy.

USER BEWARE!

The assault rifle is a solid multi-purpose weapon but you may want to look to others to help you through specific scenarios.

EXPLOSIVE WEAPONS

If you are looking to devastate buildings, crush enemies, and generally cause a whole heap of chaos, then you are going to want a Launcher in your inventory. These weapons pack a huge punch and excel at range, putting you in a power position at practically any point in the game. Plus, if you're playing with friends, you can always try to ride a rocket round the map to earn some serious respect from your fellow gamers.

BE ON THE LOOKOUT FOR THE...

◀ LEGENDARY ROCKET LAUNCHER

Rarity: Legendary **Damage:** High
Magazine Size: Low **Reload Time:** High
Damage Per Second: Medium

The Rocket Launcher is an old-school favorite.
It doesn't discriminate, decimating players and
structures in seconds.

USER BEWARE!

Epic will occasionally
Vault weapons and items,
temporarily removing
them from the game for
rebalancing.

PISTOLS

Remember, bigger doesn't always mean better. While it can be tempting to steer clear of the pistol in favor of larger weapons, they sure can pack a punch in the right situation. With their excellent rate of fire and extreme versatility, the pistol can be an excellent tool in close- and mid-range engagements, especially if you're trying to keep noise to a minimum.

◀

BE ON THE LOOKOUT FOR THE...

LEGENDARY SUPPRESSED PISTOL

Rarity: Legendary **Damage:** Low
Magazine Size: Medium **Reload Time:** Low
Damage Per Second: High

This weapon is excellent in the early and mid sections of the game, its suppressor allowing you to remain undetected as you move between areas.

USER BEWARE!

The pistol is often overlooked by some players, but it can be surprisingly effective if used in the right situation.

BOLT ACTION SNIPER RIFLES

Looking to ruin a few days from a distance? These weapons will drop enemies quickly if you're accurate and can cause epic amounts of disruption. Sniper rifles will take a lot of practice to master, particularly if you are shooting at moving targets— remember, try to anticipate where an enemy is running and shoot a little ahead of them, making sure to keep bullet drop markers on the reticule in mind if you are shooting from more than 100 yards away.

BE ON THE LOOKOUT FOR THE...

LEGENDARY HEAVY SNIPER RIFLE

Rarity: Legendary **Damage:** High
Magazine Size: Low **Reload Time:** Low
Damage Per Second: Medium

While it's slow to fire, the Bolt Action Sniper Rifle will net you easy eliminations if you can pull off a sweet headshot.

USER BEWARE!

Sniper rifles take a while to reload, so try to be confident that your shot will connect before pulling the trigger.

COMBAT TACTICS

HOW TO WIN MORE 1V1 ENCOUNTERS AND GET MORE ELIMS PER MATCH

There's more to claiming an elimination than pulling the trigger: Learning how to make the most of the tools and terrain around you is key to coming out on top. The truth is, you only need one elimination

to lay claim to a Victory Royale. However, you're going to need to get your head around some combat tactics to give you an edge against anybody that crosses your path while you're out exploring the island. One way to get ahead is to act irrationally and improvise wherever possible—that way no one can predict your next move!

KEEP CALM UNDER FIRE

Nobody likes being eliminated in Fortnite. Avoiding such a fate is easier said than done, but it would be wise to try to keep a cool head whenever you do find yourself in combat. There is never any one sure-fire way to win, so you'll want to adapt your tactics to suit the moment. If you need a second to consider your options, try laying down structures for cover and wait to see how your opponent reacts. From there, these three tips should come in handy:

SLOW DOWN AT RANGE

Don't get in a panic when entering into a long-distance duel; you don't need to jump all over the place to survive. Instead, try crouching down, look for cover, take a deep breath, and return fire with measured shots.

KEEP MOVING UP CLOSE

If you need to slow down to be effective at range, the opposite applies in close-quarters combat. Pull out a weapon with high DPS and use frantic movement patterns to disorient your aggressor.

MAINTAIN THE HIGH GROUND

Whether you're using natural points of elevation or purpose-built ramps, you should always look to get above an enemy for an easier opportunity at a headshot. Use height to your advantage!

USE THE RIGHT WEAPONS

You can never be certain what weapons you're going to end up with—you'll need to work with what you can get your hands on. The key is to ensure that you've always got your eye on creating a balanced loadout, cycling through weapons that match with the type of environment that you're in.

SLOT YOUR WEAPONS EFFECTIVELY

Fortnite is a fast-paced game, but it's well worth finding the time to keep your five inventory slots in order. Keep your weapons next to one another on the left with your medical supplies and special-use items off to the right to avoid accidentally selecting them when frantically cycling between them all in combat.

BAIT AND TRAP

Traps are often underutilized in Fortnite. Traps—such as Damage and Floor Traps—are perfect when retreating to a household or inside a hastily built fort. A great trick is to place a Damage Trap underneath a tile, then shoot it out to drop your opponent down into it. They'll never know what hit 'em.

FIRE IN SMALL BURSTS

When it comes to fully automatic weapons, your accuracy will go out the window the longer you hold down the trigger. The solid tactic is to fire in short bursts. This will negate bloom significantly and plays directly into the mantra of taking your time and reducing movement when using precision weapons.

USE BUILDS EFFECTIVELY

BE UNPREDICTABLE

Remember to utilize your ability to build on the move. Combine ramps and floor pieces to create and close distances to disorient your enemy.

HALT RAMPS

If you see a player building a ramp up to your position, simply lay a floor tile over the ramp, forcing your rival to change their tactic and go on the defensive.

USER BEWARE!

Building can be used offensively and defensively. That's why you should try to integrate structures into your tactics where possible.

PROTECT YOUR REAR

If you create a fortification be sure to find the time to build a wall behind you. That way you can counter anyone who tries to catch you off guard.

REINFORCE YOUR RAMP

Ramps are easily broken. Get into the habit of building a wall, a floor, and then a ramp above it, giving you more cover and tactical opportunities.

TEAM TACTICS

THE BEST TACTICS TO USE WHEN PLAYING IN A DUO OR SQUAD

The foundations for success are very much the same for solo and squad play in Fortnite, but there are a few special considerations that you should be aware of when playing with a group. You need to work together, use clear lines of communication in an effort to unleash advanced tactical maneuvers, call out enemy threats on the horizon, and argue over who is going to pick up the Legendary Assault Rifle drop. So, to ensure you're making the most of your allies in the battlefield, we've gathered together some integral tactics for teamwork and group play.

WORK AS A UNIT

Playing with others is all about coordination. The first real test for any group of players is the Battle Bus—before leaping out you'll want to settle on a landing location. Look to jump into the fray together and quickly push toward the pre-agreed coordinates. Follow these basics if you want to counter any threats that you may come across in the early game when working as a unit.

USE YOUR COMPASS

Running along the top of your screen is a compass. Get into the habit of calling out enemy positions and incoming fire by way of compass coordinates. It's a great shorthand.

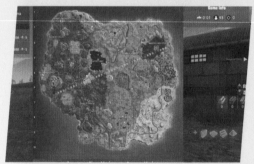

USE PLAYER MARKERS

Every player in your squad can lay down a marker on the map. These are integral for keeping your team together, particularly if one of the group isn't using voice chat. Keep the map updated so the squad knows which direction to move in.

USE CLEAR COMMUNICATION

You should look to use the voice communication features in Fortnite to maintain clear lines of communication with your squad. Identify weapons, enemies, and points of interest on the horizon.

USER BEWARE!

The benefit of playing with others is that you all get to experience the chaos! Play nice, play together, and remember to have fun.

SHARING IS CARING

It's important to share resources, items, and duties in group play. Remember, a better-geared team will ultimately have a better chance at claiming a Victory Royale. Share Small Shields, hand off Rare weapons if they are needed elsewhere, and make sure you're all sharing harvesting material responsibilities together.

GIVE YOUR FRIENDS SOME SPACE

If you're covering large amounts of terrain or clearing up areas, it would be wise to spread yourselves out. Groups that bunch up make themselves a bigger target, and are easily susceptible to being flanked from rival teams. Sure, keep eyes on your squad when you can, but a little breathing room isn't the worst thing in the world.

DON'T RUSH DOWNED PLAYERS

It can be tempting to pounce on an enemy player who has been downed. Instead you should hold back, train your crosshairs on the fallen, and use them as bait when the opposing group rushes in to try and save their buddy. Once the entire squad is accounted for, your group should then look to go in and overwhelm.

ONLY REVIVE WHEN IT'S SAFE

When you're playing as a team you have the benefit of being able to revive members of your squad. It can take time, so you need to be prepared to lay down covering fire as your buddy crawls to safety, or your squad need to be prepared to create quick build cover to reach the fallen without putting yourselves at risk.

USE FLANKING CAREFULLY

If you get caught in a direct confrontation with a rival group across a small or mid-range distance, look to divide and conquer. While your squad lays down covering fire, you should look to move in an arc to the left or right of your aggressors, using the terrain to help conceal your movement.

FOCUS ON DIVIDED TEAMS

Flanking can be a risky business. It effectively means you're dividing your group, and you're always at your weakest when your duo or squad is separated. If you flank and it goes wrong, you'll need to regroup as fast as possible. On the flipside, if you see a team that's split up, concentrate your fire on one player at a time.

BLENDING IN

HOW TO USE THE ENVIRONMENT TO AVOID DETECTION

While it can be really tempting to fight every player you come across in Fortnite, it isn't absolutely necessary—there's a far quieter route to reaching the final 20 bracket. It involves avoiding altercations, sticking to the shadows, and using everything in your arsenal to blend into the

environment. Fortnite can be a game of action, but there's also the opportunity to play it much slower and more considerately if that's your style. Blending in is all about getting your head down, keeping it simple with your Outfits, and becoming best friends with those green bushes that you've no doubt noticed across the island. There's plenty you can do to help turn the tide in your favor...but, like, just keep that between us, okay? It's our sneaky little secret.

HIDE IN PLAIN SIGHT

Fortnite gives you the tools to be super stealthy, so embrace them! One way of disguising yourself is to find the Legendary Bush consumable item out in the field; it's one of the best ways to move around without anybody immediately spotting you. If you aren't so lucky to get one in a chest, try wearing a camo-colored skin and crouch down in any bushes you come across—unobservant players won't pay it (or you) a second look.

BUILD WITH CAUTION

While building may indeed be an excellent way of traversing the island, the truth is, it will likely signify your position to everyone in the area. If you're looking to blend into the environment and avoid altercations, you want to focus on playing as quietly as physically possible. Build as a means of survival.

KEEP IT SIMPLE

The struggle of choosing between an Outfit that will allow you to express yourself and one that can help you blend into the environment is real. Still, try to pair your Outfit with the part of the map that you are more likely to head towards on the island—we've all got our favorite locations, after all!

TAKE IT SLOW

It can be all too tempting to start running for your life the second your boots hit the ground. That, friends, is how you get spotted and shot. If you want to play it safe, you should stay crouched when you can, moving slowly between points of cover and avoiding altercations where possible.

KEEP MOVING

As you move across the island you'll no doubt find it pretty tempting to raid houses for loot. Consider prioritizing single-storey houses to duck into. These small buildings are quick to gut of all materials, can often contain a chest, and will be easy enough to escape from should trouble come knocking!

CONSIDER THE SNIPER RIFLE

While blending in and playing stealthily is about reducing your noise and footprint as much as possible, you should always be ready to strike should the opportunity present itself. Consider bringing a sniper rifle along with you to track and—if you're up to it—eliminate other players at a distance.

PROCEED WITH CAUTION

CLOSE DOORS BEHIND YOU

If you're trying to keep a low profile, you may want to consider closing doors behind you as you enter buildings. It'll help reduce your visibility.

GRAB SILENCED WEAPONS

Weapons equipped with silencers can be found across the island and these will help reduce the amount of noise you make while claiming eliminations.

GATHER MATERIALS CAREFULLY

It's important to gather materials as you approach the late game but be wary of how much noise you may make as you begin smashing cars and trees.

RESPOND QUICKLY

One thing to keep in mind while trying to blend in is the need to respond quickly to threats and situations as they unravel in front of you.

ITEMS GUIDE

THE NON-COMBATIVE STRATEGIES YOU NEED TO MASTER

Sometimes you need to get a little improvisational to come out
on top. Sure, you may have found a Legendary Assault Rifle, but
that won't do you a lot of good when you're staring down the

business end of well-placed trap. There are various pathways to victory, and they don't always involve eliminating the competition by conventional means—sometimes you don't even need to fire a single shot. While some of these gadgets can be hard to come by in the course of natural play, we are going lay out a few reasons why you should be prepared to throw down a weapon or consumable in an effort to introduce items into your inventory.

STICKY SITUATION

Many overlook the Sticky Grenade, but it has far more utility than many give it credit for. While it can be used as a trap, it can also be used by skilled players to cause total humiliation. If a rival gets knocked, try sticking the Clinger on their person so the team rushing in to revive them gets caught unawares.

THE TRAP BOX

It's possible to take a player out of a game with such grace that they will be left speechless. One such way is by making use of the trap box. You'll need to lure an enemy into close-quarters combat before quickly throwing up walls around them, effectively holding them in place, before then chucking a trap into the fray.

LET'S BOOGIE

Who can resist a little dance-off? Boogie Bombs may not deal direct damage to rival players, but they do an excellent job of incapacitating them. Catch an enemy with one of these, and they will be whipped into an uncontrollable dancing frenzy, giving you plenty of time to get in close and finish them off.

BOUNCE AND LAUNCH

Movement is a key deterrent to elimination in Fortnite. This is especially true when combining Launch Pads with a Bounce Pad. Place a Bounce Pad on a wall with a Launch Pad in front. Run into the Launch Pad for momentum before being blasted up and away, moving you onto a trajectory that few can follow or defend against.

SEVEN ITEMS TO HELP YOU IMPROVISE

When things get hairy, sometimes weapons won't save you. You have to think better. Craftier. Here is just a small selection of items that can help catapult you toward victory; while many of these may not directly lead to you claiming an elimination, they could get you out of a tight spot or help you in locking down a good position on the island.

GRAPPLER

The Grappler is one of those items that can completely change the composition of an encounter. This gadget will let you latch onto distant buildings before winching yourself up to new heights, allowing you to get the drop on unsuspecting victims.

RIFT-TO-GO

Need to get somewhere fast? The Rift-To-Go has your back, letting you throw a rift down anywhere with one button press. You can jump through one to get to safety in a particularly difficult encounter, or force enemies into it with a perfectly timed deployment.

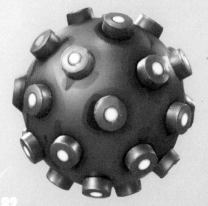

IMPULSE GRENADE

If you are looking to create an almighty distraction, you might want to give the Impulse Grenade a try. This thing does huge Area of Effect (AOE) damage, and that's something most want to avoid.

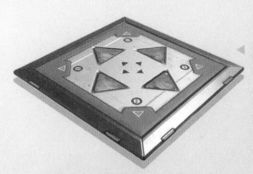

BOUNCER TRAP

This Floor Trap can boost enemies up and away from you, launch them off of walls, and act as a general annoyance. Set them anywhere you please for an easy way to push people off your trail.

PORT-A-FORT

This Rare gadget will let you deploy the perfect fort structure in seconds. Not only has this completely changed the dynamic of structure creation, giving new players the ability to build with the best of them, but if you time it just right you can pop the Port-A-Fort on top of another player, eliminating them in the process.

ALL TERRAIN KART

Zip across the battlefield in this vehicle that can tackle any terrain. Head to Lazy Links or Paradise Palms to hop in a kart that'll take you all the way across the map and away from enemies in record time.

STICKY GRENADE

If you can find the right time to use it, the Sticky Grenade will easily be one of the best gadgets in your arsenal. It's awesome for toppling structures, blowing ATKs off the road, and disorienting others in the blast vicinity.

BUILDING GUIDE
LEARN HOW TO BUILD STRUCTURES AND COVER

The real battle can be in the building. If you want to give yourself
a competitive edge you should be eager to learn this vital in-game
skill. If you can effectively and elegantly unleash structures you may

just find that you have a bit of an advantage when compared to the competition. In this section we will go over how to effectively edit tiles, create cover while under fire, erect towers that can give you maximum control over an area, and plenty more. Building will take some time to master but it's well worth getting comfortable with this side of the game if you're eager to earn a Victory Royale and dazzle your friends with your crafting competency.

BUILDING CAN BE KEY

Mastering the building mechanics inside Fortnite isn't key to a successful run at a Victory Royale. However, these tools can open up new tactical opportunities, giving you the freedom to take the fight to your enemies. Don't believe us? Here are three reasons you should consider taking the time to master your craft:

◄ CREATE YOUR OWN COVER

Rather than taking refuge in an existing building or behind a tree when you are under fire, you can create your own cover in an instant when using the building options. This tactic puts you in control of your own destiny.

SCOPE OUT AREAS ►

You should learn how to build combat towers quickly, as this will give you the ability to make intermittent scans of the surrounding area. This will help you to make tactical decisions based on any and all potential threats collecting around you.

◄ USE HEIGHT TO YOUR ADVANTAGE

Elevation will give you the upper hand in almost every combat situation Fortnite will throw at you. You should, however, be aware of your silhouette, as building too high will leave you more susceptible to ranged attacks.

CONSIDER YOUR OPTIONS

While stone and metal structures are sturdier than those made of wood, they take a lot longer to build. No two encounters are ever the same, so try to tailor your buildings to the situation at hand. If you're in need of greater protection, stone and metal structures will certainly provide it, but if you're in need of a quick solution to a problem at hand you may want to consider using wood builds.

BUILD AND RUN

You should try to treat construction as yet another weapon in your arsenal. For this to be effective you may want to try building while in motion, continually dropping new wall, ramp, stair and ceiling pieces as you figure out a way to permanently break the line of sight—or get a height advantage—over your foe. Building is an excellent way to buy some time as you prepare for your next move.

DON'T FORGET TO REPAIR

When you're caught up in the chaos of a firefight, it can be all too easy to forget that you can repair your builds, saving precious resources and time. If you can maintain repairs on a key piece of cover, not only will you stay protected, but it could force your assailant into a situation in which they need to reload, giving you the perfect opportunity to pop out of cover and nail them.

EDIT BUILDING TILES

Did you know you can customize your own structures, allowing you to finesse your work? Stand close to one of your builds and you will see the Edit prompt. Guide your cursor across the tiles that you wish to change; remove single mid-height blocks from walls to create windows or two tiles in a vertical row to create a functioning door. Experiment with what works for you.

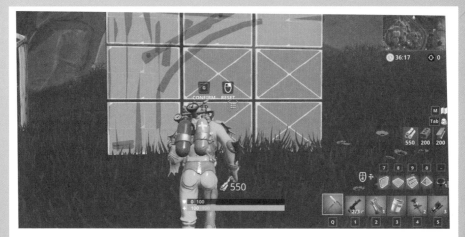

EDIT ON THE MOVE

It is possible to edit build pieces while on the move, saving you precious time in the middle of a firefight or while rushing out of the circle and into safety. While sprinting, try pulling up the build menu and dragging the cursor across the tiles you wish to edit. This is perfect for quickly manipulating ramps and walls as required.

KNOW WHEN NOT TO BUILD

Building large structures in an open space is a good way to signal your exact location, although this can have its advantages. Consider whether laying down a structure is absolutely necessary. If in doubt, utilize existing buildings for cover or crouch-walk at the foot of hills, trees, and rocks until enemies reveal themselves or you come up with another plan.

TOP-LEVEL STRUCTURAL EDITING

Expert builders are capable of editing their own structures while building around others that are in pursuit. Stay aware of where your opponent is at all times and attempt to lay pieces around them. To get next-level with this, try removing a wall piece before quickly throwing a trap into the mix and sealing up the only exit. This will leave your foe with nowhere to go but the spectator screen.

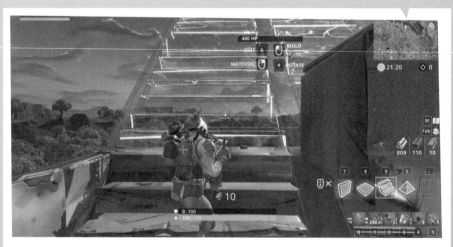

ROOM TO BREATHE

Getting caught by someone mid-heal can often put a sudden end to any Battle Royale session. In the mid-to-late game, you should try to heal inside box structures with a flat roof. When you're ready to move on, construct a ramp and remove half of the flat roof before placing another ramp ahead so you can begin building upward safely with your behind protected.

BUILD AGGRESSIVELY

As the aggressor, you'll control how enemies interact with you, and will often be able to force them into awkward positions. Be confident in your building ability, and don't be afraid to build toward others. Try using ramps and walls to disorient your enemies and, when in doubt, build tall structures to gain a height advantage.

PRACTICE BUILDING FREQUENTLY

Learning how to build from muscle memory, even with other players bearing down on your position, takes time and patience. Try heading into Playground Mode before starting up a Battle Royale session to practice without the pressure. Doing this will give you the time and space to improve your building times, and you can even bring in a friend to help simulate a 1v1 confrontation.

ESSENTIAL BUILDS

Here, you'll find a handpicked selection of builds that can really help to elevate your survival skills and offensive capabilities to the next level. These simple creations can often be the difference between life and elimination in Battle Royale.

THE BOX ▶

This simple 1x1 structure is the bedrock to all of Fortnite's building. Bring up the Build menu and drop four walls as you swivel in place—make sure that you have Quick Build turned on in the Options menu. This will provide basic protection while you heal or gather loot from a fallen enemy. If you want, drop a ramp allowing you to peek over the edge and gain a small amount of elevation over any approaching enemies.

◄ SNIPER'S NEST

This is essentially a variant of the tower, but it's fantastic in Squad Mode for giving your entire team the ability to rule over a section of the map from the sky. Start by building a 2x2 box before placing edited pyramid pieces into each of the corners and stairs, protruding outwards from the main walls. You are effectively creating a building that looks as if it is funneling you inwards. Repeat this a second time to gain elevation, and the funnel will be large enough to house your entire team, giving you plenty of cover and authority over the ground.

◄ THE TOWER

This is an essential of the late game. Begin by constructing the 1x1 box. Next, stand on the ramp and jump to place another floor, then a ramp. Continue alternating between these two tiles to gain height. Finish off with another box at the top of the tower for added protection. Be wary of building too high up, as this could give away your position to other players.

▲ REINFORCED DOUBLE RAMP

Once you reach the mid-to-late game, you are going to want to use ramps to get around—either to quickly close distances between you and other players, or to easily reach higher planes of elevation. Place two ramps side by side, and then erect a wall behind each ramp to give it some added reinforcement it, which should give it some protection from small-arms fire. Try including floor pieces in this build for added protection.

93

VEHICLES GUIDE

GET INTO FORTNITE'S MOST EXCITING NEW ADDITION

Getting around the island with your feet is *so* Season 3. If you're looking to tackle traversal with style, you'll want to think about getting your hands on a vehicle. It doesn't matter whether you're

rolling solo or with a few buddies by your side, these four Rare finds will bring a new dynamic to your play. For groups, a vehicle creates the opportunity to turn your squad into a roving elimination machine; for solo players, it'll give you a little more flexibility in your approach to deadly situations and attempts to outrun the circle. While vehicles can be difficult to find, they have the capability to completely change your ability to outmaneuver an otherwise impossible obstacle.

VEHICLES ARE RARE FINDS

Vehicles are powerful and potentially game-changing items in the right hands. That means you're going to need to put some effort into seeking them out. Check dark corners for the Shopping Cart, Outposts for the X4-Stormwing, and outside of RVs for the Quadcrasher and ATK.

REACH FOR THE SKY

The Quadcrasher will build up its boost capabilities so long as there is somebody behind the wheel. Take the vehicle off of a ramp or structure while boosting to get massive airtime. If you pull back on the stick, you'll be able to increase your hang-time, covering even more ground across the island.

REMEMBER TO SWITCH SEATS

You can make the X4-Stormwing a viable weapon in solo play. If you spot an enemy that you want to disrupt, try levelling out the vehicle and clicking in the right stick to switch seats from the cockpit to the wing—as you switch, whip out a weapon and claim an elimination before jumping back behind the wheel.

BOOST FTW

To speed up your journey across the island, remember to use the ATK's boost functionality; if you kick into a drift by using the handbrake, you'll start seeing sparks fly from the wheels—blue denotes a small boost, yellow is a medium boost, and red sparks are for a long boost.

WELCOME TO THE GARAGE

It's up to you how you want to utilize them, but vehicles are an exciting part of Fortnite that can turn games on their head. Work with your squad to find new and interesting ways to incorporate them into your tactics, and solo players should look to find new ways to integrate vehicles into your play to help drive you straight into the end game.

◀ ALL TERRAIN KART

If you come across the All Terrain Kart with your squad you should think of it as an excellent way to cruise the island with all of your buddies in tow. For you solo players out there, the ATK is not only fantastic for outrunning the Storm but it can also be used as a weapon should you get the handling down. While the ATK may lack subtlety it sure is an awesome way of covering ground quickly.

QUADCRASHER ▶

The Quadcrasher is a form of total destruction. Seating two players, this vehicle becomes more dangerous the longer you are behind the wheel, steadily building up boost over time. Get enough speed and you'll find that it can smash through just about anything—players, structures, you name it! This ride can be difficult to locate, but it's worth putting the time and energy in to do so.

X-4 STORMWING

The first flying vehicle introduced to Fortnite, the X-4 Stormwing is a strong and speedy ticket to getting you (and your friends!) a little closer to that Victory Royale you so desperately crave. It's about four times faster than sprinting and has enough room for you and four other players; featuring an airbrake, boost, and a mounted machine gun, the X-4 Stormwing is the fastest form of transportation and—in the right hands—also one of the most disruptive. It'll be tough to find, but it's worth the effort.

USER BEWARE!

Fortnite is constantly changing, so don't be surprised if some of the capabilities of the various vehicles changes over time.

SHOPPING CART ▶

The Shopping Cart was the first vehicle introduced to Fortnite and it is still a viable alternative to, you know, walking with your own two feet. If you're running solo, taking the Shopping Cart for a spin may leave you susceptible to attacks. If you're rolling with a partner, on the other hand, you'll be able to shepherd them around in the cage—becoming a mobile attack force that will send other players reeling.

TRUE OR FALSE!

FORTNITE'S MYTHS—DEBUNKED

Listen, you shouldn't believe everything that you read on the
Internet. As fun as a fool's errand can be, there's enough chaos to
be found in Battle Royale without pouring your time into attempting

the impossible. That's why we wanted to take this opportunity to look into some of the biggest Fortnite myths. Can you really ride a rocket? Is it possible to survive the Storm indefinitely? Can you groove your way back to full health? We'll answer all of this and more as we attempt to debunk some of Fortnite's biggest myths.

FALSE!

CERTAIN EMOTES HELP YOU HEAL FASTER!

So, once upon a time, there was a glitch that enabled players to use the Rock, Paper, Scissors emote to cancel the time needed to use a Bandage while still getting all the benefits. Of course, it didn't take long for this to pop up online and for your friends here at Epic Games to get that patched out of existence. Rumors have long persisted that you can indeed dance yourself to better health. The truth is, it just isn't possible. So, regardless of how many sweet moves you bust, no emotes will enable you to remove the application timer on a Bandage or Small Shield. You're just going to have to find some place to hide when under fire like everybody else.

YOU RUN FASTER WITHOUT A WEAPON EQUIPPED!

FALSE!

One of the oldest myths in the game, and one that persists to this day, is the belief that your running speed is affected by the weapon that you're carrying. The truth is, it doesn't matter whether you've got a Harvesting Tool in hand or if you are slinging around a minigun, you're not going to move any faster or slower because of it.

YOU CAN DEFINITELY RIDE ROCKETS ACROSS THE MAP!

TRUE!

Is there anything deadlier in Battle Royale than a player wielding a Legendary Assault Rifle blasting across the map atop a Guided Missile? As it happens, no! The projectiles launched out of a Guided Missile Launcher are indeed large enough to carry a player, creating some truly ingenious tactical maneuvers. It's difficult to pull off, but it is absolutely possible to do so (plus you'll look super cool while you're doing it).

THERE ARE WAYS TO SURVIVE IN THE STORM!

FALSE!

Ah, the electrical damage of the Storm. It's the feature of Fortnite that catches everybody off guard, eventually. But what if you could survive in the life-sapping Storm? You'd have a huge tactical advantage, right? Well, we're sorry to burst your—ahem—bubble, but the rumors of using a Chug Jug while half in/half out of the Storm and the like are totally bogus. You're just going to have to avoid the Storm like everybody else.

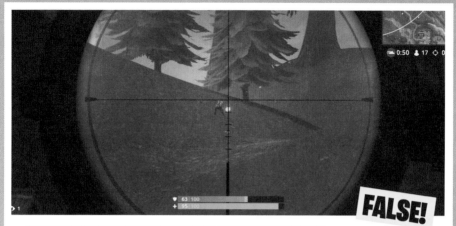

DIFFERENT OUTFITS HAVE DIFFERENT HIT BOXES!

While Fortnite does have a huge variety of Outfits for players to wear, this has made certain corners of the community peddle the belief that these skins possess subtly different hit boxes. Are you less of a target if you're a Renegade Raider as opposed to a Creepy Bear? One does have a much larger head than the other. Well, that wouldn't be fair, now, would it? The hit boxes on each skin are exactly the same.

LANDING ON A SLOPE CANCELS FALL DAMAGE!

Fall damage is the bane of many a player, with a misjudged drop robbing you of your HP when you need it the most. Problem is, fall damage is an imprecise science, so it's allowed for all manner of theories that landing at certain angles on a slope can actively reduce the damage it causes. In reality, though, it's a total roll of the dice.

V-BUCKS AND THE BATTLE PASS

EVERYTHING YOU NEED TO KNOW ABOUT FORTNITE'S IN-GAME CURRENCY AND REWARD SYSTEM

When it comes to Fortnite, it's V-Bucks that make the world go round. Have you seen your friends running about in outrageous Outfits, grooving their hearts out with an array of killer dance moves? That's because they've been spending their V-Bucks wisely. If you want to look far cooler than the competition as you mercilessly eliminate them one by one in Battle Royale, you're going to want to fill your virtual wallet with V-Bucks.

HOW TO GET V-BUCKS

V-Bucks are a virtual currency that can be used for purchasing items from the in-game store, such as Outfits and emotes. It will also enable you to get your hands on the Premium Battle Pass. Every item in Battle Royale that can be purchased with V-Bucks is strictly cosmetic and will have no effect on gameplay.

BUY THEM

You can purchase V-Bucks with your real-world dollars in bundles of 1,000, 2,500, 6,000, and 10,000. Also be on the lookout for starter packs, which will often bundle V-Bucks in with seasonal Outfits. Always ask permission from the registered card holder before you make any purchases.

COMPLETE CHALLENGES

You can earn bundles of V-Bucks by reaching the lower reward tiers of each season. Focus on completing daily and event challenges to get yourself some free V-Bucks. Perfect for obtaining new Outfits without spending a dime.

MOVE UP THE RANKS

If you purchase the Premium Battle Pass, you will find V-Bucks distributed all throughout the seasonal reward tiers. In many ways, the Battle Pass is the road to Fortnite's greatest rewards, including a wallet full of V-Bucks.

GET THE BATTLE PASS

Most of Fortnite's unlockable items are tied to each season's Battle Pass, at both a free and premium paid level. V-Bucks are offered all across the reward tiers, so the 950 V-Bucks is but a small price of entry to pay. The more Fortnite you play and the more challenges that you complete with your friends, the faster you'll find yourself with a bunch of awesome seasonal rewards!

DEDICATE TIME

The most dedicated of Fortnite players—those who spend their time completing daily, weekly, and Battle Pass challenges—will find that they'll quickly be inundated with exclusive Outfits and emotes. For example, Season 7's Battle Pass will let you earn up to 100 rewards worth over 25,000 V-Bucks—that would typically take up to 150 hours of normal play to earn!

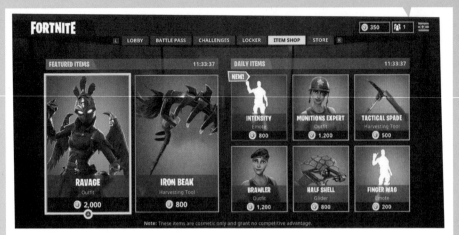

AVOID FREE V-BUCKS SCAMS

The only place you can purchase V-Bucks is through Epic. Don't believe the scammers, social media giveaways, or any other nonsense you might read online. If you're after V-Bucks, you'll either have to earn them the old-fashioned way (leveling up through the Battle Pass), or by exchanging money for virtual coins through the Fortnite storefront.

TRY SAVE THE WORLD

Fortnite's Save the World PvE campaign makes it easy to earn large amounts of V-Bucks without spending your real-world money, which you can then carry across to your Battle Royale experience. By completing story missions, challenges, daily quests—and even just by logging in!—in Save the World, you may just find your pockets lined with V-Bucks in no time.

COLLABORATE WITH FRIENDS

The Battle Pass will occasionally hand out Friend XP Boosts, which can be used to help your entire squad level up a little quicker. Not only will this make you the favorite member of your friend group, it also means you'll get through the Battle Pass ranks a little quicker—giving you yet another opportunity to get your hands on those free V-Bucks before the season ends.

Cataloguing in Publication Data is available from the British Library

Hardback 978 14722 6213 4

Design by Future plc.

All images © Epic Games, Inc.

Printed and bound in Italy by L.E.G.O. S.p.A.

HEADLINE PUBLISHING GROUP

An Hachette UK Company
Carmelite House
50 Victoria Embankment
London, EC4 0DZ
www.headline.co.uk www.hachette.co.uk

Little, Brown and Company
Hachette Book Group
1290 Avenue of the Americas, New York, NY 10104
Visit us at LBYR.com

www.epicgames.com

First Edition: April 2019

First U.S. Edition: May 2019

Little, Brown and Company is a division of
Hachette Book Group, Inc.

The Little, Brown name and logo are trademarks of
Hachette Book Group, Inc.

Library of Congress Control Number: 2018957940

ISBNs: 978-0-316-49126-6 (paper over board)
978-0-316-49128-0 (ebook), 978-0-316-49125-9 (ebook),
978-0-316-49133-4 (ebook)

U.S. Edition printed in the United States of America

All images © Epic Games, Inc.

WOR

UK Hardback: 10 9 8 7 6 5 4 3 2 1
U.S. Paper Over Board: 10 9 8 7 6 5 4 3 2 1